THE LIT
CLE
TIPS

WILLIAM FORTT

THE LITTLE BOOK OF CLEANING TIPS

WILLIAM FORTT

A.
Absolute Press

First published in Great Britain in 2013 by
Absolute Press, an imprint of Bloomsbury Publishing Plc
Scarborough House, 29 James Street West
Bath BA1 2BT, England
Phone +44 (0)1225 316013 **Fax** +44 (0)1225 445836
E-mail info@absolutepress.co.uk
Web www.absolutepress.co.uk

A catalogue record of this book is available from the British Library
ISBN 13: 9781906650933
Printed and bound by Hung Hing, China.

Bloomsbury Publishing Plc
50 Bedford Square, London WC1B 3DP | www.bloomsbury.com

‘I hate housework. You make the beds,
you do the dishes and six months later
you have to start all over again.’

Joan Rivers (b. 1933),
American comedian and actor

1

Keep a sense of perspective about cleaning.

Some things (sinks, lavatories, kitchen work surfaces) need to be kept scrupulously clean for hygienic reasons. Others (bath taps, shelves, brass candlesticks) can survive a little dirt, even if they look scruffy. If you're pushed for time, just concentrate on the essentials.

2

Tidiness is the basis of cleanliness.

A tidy house is much easier to keep clean than a shambles. Get things put in their proper drawers and cupboards and boxes instead of littering the floor, and ruthlessly bin or recycle rubbish or unwanted items.

3

Stay on top of the washing.

Dirty clothes and dishes are unavoidable features of life, so avoid a backlog. When you've got enough for a full washing machine, set it going at once. And do the washing up straight away rather than leaving crocks to marinate in their own filth overnight.

4

Keep cleaning liquids separate. There is a huge variety of powerful chemicals in polishes, detergents, solvents and the rest. They don't often improve with mixing together – in fact some combinations, such as chlorine bleach and acidic toilet cleaners, can produce lethal fumes.

Read the labels carefully to avoid disaster.

5

Natural wood worktops and chopping boards can pick up **odours from onions, meat, fish** and other foods, which even hot water and soap can't disperse. Rub these surfaces with half a lemon to get rid of these smells, then wipe over with a warm, damp, clean cloth.

6

Keep a bottle of **uncoloured malt or cider vinegar handy.**

It's a cheap, natural and environmentally friendly cleaner with an amazing number of uses. Vinegar clears away dirt and grease. It removes nasty odours and bath tide marks. It dissolves limescale from kettles, shower heads and taps. And you can use it in the wash instead of fabric conditioner.

7

Do your dusting from the top. If you're dusting a room with a cloth or a wool duster, start with the highest places – ceiling lights, picture rails, pictures, window frames and so on.

Always work downwards.

That way you drive the dust to the floor, where it can easily be collected by the vacuum cleaner.

8

Dust furniture with a slightly damp cloth.

A dry cloth is not very effective at picking up dust particles. It will also drag the dirt over the thing you're trying to clean, possibly scratching it. Spray a little water on the cloth, so it will slide better over the surfaces. For wooden furniture, move the duster in the direction of the grain.

9

Deal with blood stains before they can dry. Mix up a **paste of cornflour and water** (talcum powder and water is an alternative). Spread this on the fresh blood spots and leave to dry naturally. The cornflour will absorb the blood. When it's dry, simply brush off with a nail brush or soft scrubbing brush.

10

Smelly musty carpet? Your carpet can be clean yet still pong a bit – especially if you've got a dog. Sprinkle baking soda sparingly all over the carpet last thing at night (but keep pets well away). The soda will absorb the mustiness and other odours. Next morning, vacuum it all thoroughly.

11

The **slats of blinds** collect dust, yet they can be fiddly to clean. **Get an old pair of socks** and slip one on your cleaning hand. Use this to wipe the dust off the slats. Then swap socks, wetting the second one with soapy water to clean the blind more thoroughly. Turn the sock round, and use the dry side to dry and polish.

12

White sliced bread has one redeeming feature – you can use it **to clean oil paintings** which aren't too precious. Cut off the crust and squash the slice into a ball. Very gently dab or roll this on the surface of the painting. You'll be amazed by how much dirt it will soak up. Brush off the crumbs with a soft paintbrush. Not recommended for Old Masters.

13

Give your kitchen sink drain a good sluice out once a month. Chuck a handful of baking soda down the plughole, followed by a slosh of cider vinegar. The result will be a dramatic but cathartic fizzing and bubbling. After half an hour, rinse out the sink with cold water.

14

If you **spill food on the oven hob, wipe it up immediately.**

Messing up the cooker is one of the natural by-products of cooking. But if you clean up right away, the blobs and splats won't have time to get baked on hard. The trickier areas (round the burners, for example) will have to wait until the cooker has cooled down.

15

Filthy, encrusted pots and dishes?

Save your elbow grease for other jobs, and fill the kitchen sink with hot water. Dissolve one dishwasher tablet in it, then submerge the troublesome pans and leave for a good soak overnight. Next morning all the assorted muck should be easy to rinse off.

16

Washing-up Basics #1: Hot Water Is Best. Some swear by cold, but hot water really kills germs, and shifts congealed fats and other gunk. A good eco-friendly detergent, in moderation, also helps. After washing, rinse off in clean hot water – or cold, if you must. If the water is really hot, protect your hands with rubber gloves.

17

Use wooden chopping boards instead of plastic ones.

Wood contains several natural substances, such as tannin and vanillin, which discourage the growth of harmful bacteria. In other words, as long as you wash and wipe them regularly, they're pretty safe. Plastic, by contrast, has no natural defences and bacteria can grow freely.

18

Cleanse shower curtains and non-slip mats regularly to stop mould and worse. Wash them in the bath with warm water and laundry liquid, and rinse thoroughly. Then hang to dry in a warm (but not hot) place or, better still, outside.

19

Washing-up Basics #2: Order of Battle.

Start with the least dirty utensils, such as glasses and coffee mugs, while the water's cleanest. Move on to plates and bowls, rinsing off the worst deposits under the cold tap first. After this, wash the cutlery (also rinsed first) and end up with the muckiest baking trays, saucepans and dishes.

20

The classic way to **clean fresh red wine stains from a carpet** is to pour white wine over it. However, it's cheaper to use soda water. Leave for five minutes and blot with a cloth. If this doesn't work, more drastic measures may be needed – soak with carpet shampoo, glycerine and water or, as a last resort, meths.

21

To get **Blu-Tack, plasticine or chewing gum out of a carpet,**

first scrape away the worst with a blunt knife. Then put ice cubes on the rest. The frozen gunge will be brittle, and can be chipped away. Any stains left should be treated (gently) with methylated spirits.

22

Candle wax on the table or the wall?

Remove it by turning your iron to a low heat, covering the wax with a piece of kitchen paper or a clean cloth, and warming it gently with the iron. As the wax melts, it will soak into the paper. Before it is scorched by the iron, replace with a fresh piece or area of the cloth.

23

Here are just two of **the many and surprising wonders of hairspray.** You can use it to kill flies. And you can spray it on walls and other surfaces to help remove magic marker scribbles. Plus, of course, you can fix your hair with it.

24

When washing towels, omit the fabric conditioner.

This tends to build up in the thick fibres over time, and can make the towels feel stiff. They may also smell mouldy. If your towels are in this condition, wash them without any laundry liquid at all at 40°C minimum and dry in the open air if possible.

25

Clean glasses fast and well the professional way.

Have ready a sink of hot water and washing-up liquid, plus a basin with hot water and a little wine vinegar. Take the glass by the base and plunge up and down in the soapy water. Then rinse in the vinegary water. Drain upside down on a clean tea towel on the draining board.

26

Wear thin rubber gloves when you wash up glasses and cups. Run your finger and thumb round the rims firmly but carefully before rinsing.

This will **remove the stubborn traces of lipstick or lip salve.**

27

The outside of windows can get very dusty. Put water on them, and you're just producing mud which will smear. So, **before you wash the windows,** remove the worst of the muck from the panes, glazing bars and sills with a soft brush that will get into the corners.

28

Choose a cloudy day for cleaning your windows. Hot sun dries the liquid too fast and encourages streakiness. Dip a cotton cloth into cleaning solution and rub away the surface dirt on the windows. Dry and polish up with a bladed squeegee, or – cheaper and simpler – with balled up sheets of newspaper.

29

To get rid of rotten food smells in the fridge, first wipe the fridge out with a damp cloth dotted with freshly squeezed lemon juice. Then pour a little vanilla essence onto a piece of cotton wool, place on a small dish and pop it inside for a few days. It also helps if you get rid of food before it starts decaying.

30

Dogs and cats inevitably shed hairs. Happily, some brands of vacuum cleaner (such as Miele) have a specialised nozzle to deal with these. Lacking this, you can employ the traditional method of wrapping sticky tape round your fingers, sticky side out, and dabbing them up. Change the tape frequently.

31

Washing-up Basics #3: Draining and Drying.

The hotter the water, the quicker the stuff will dry. Stack plates and pots on end, so the water can drain away, rather than on top of each other. Put cutlery, also on end, in a separate drainer. Recruit a willing and well-coordinated wiper-upper or – even better – two.

32

Chair and table legs can leave **dents in the carpet. Get rid of these** by rubbing an ice cube in the dent. Leave the spot to dry, then raise the nap of the carpet again with a stiff brush. And, of course, move the offending furniture an inch or two sideways.

33

If you spill emulsion or gloss paint on the carpet, clean up as soon as possible, before it dries. Use a spoon or spatula to scoop up the excess. Sponge an emulsion spill with cold water, adding some carpet shampoo if necessary. Gloss paint is oil based, so sponge with plenty of white spirit (though this can affect the fabric colour). Rinse with warm soapy water.

34

Treat cast-iron grill pans and frying pans with respect.

Keep them away from the dishwasher and ferocious cleaning fluids. The aim is to avoid rust and build up a non-stick patina. So, once cured from new (see the instructions), wash the pan in warm soapy water. Scrape away gunge with a plastic spatula. Rinse thoroughly and dry immediately.

35

Always store glasses upright. There are several good reasons for this. If you store them upside down, the air inside is trapped and goes stale. At the same time, the rim of the glass is in contact with the shelf, which may not be very clean. Thirdly, the rim is the most vulnerable part of the glass, and may be damaged inadvertently.

36

Avoid furniture sprays where possible. Unlike ordinary polishes whose solvent evaporates, sprays are based on silicone, which doesn't. Overuse will lead to a sticky, white and unpleasant build-up, which is no use for cherished wooden furniture. Instead, rub in a proper furniture polish or – if you really care – a good quality wax.

37

Go easy with grease stains on clothes or furnishings.

The immediate reaction is to rub with detergent, which spreads the stain even further. First of all, dab away as much grease as possible with paper towels. Then drip on a little detergent (laundry or washing-up liquid) and rub in gently with a fingertip. Wait ten minutes and rinse with hot water.

38

An oil stain which has dried out can be hard to shift. Give it a squirt of WD40, and leave for ten minutes. The spray will mix with the oil and moisten it. You can now proceed with the steps for grease stains outlined in the preceding tip.

39

The glass of woodburning stoves is easily sooted over.

When the stove is cool, clean the glass with balls of newspaper dipped in the wood ashes. For some reason, this works amazingly well. For stubborn bits, use a damp cloth also dipped in ash. Make sure the glass is dry before you light the stove again.

40

Clean your own chimney.

Properly fitted woodburners have a metal flue, which is easy to clean (if you have brushes). Open the door, remove the baffle plate and locate the flue opening. Shove the brush up, screw on the next cane, shove up and repeat – always twisting the whole thing clockwise – till it emerges from the top. Pull it all down again.

41

Deal with mice as quickly as possible –

they multiply very fast and are a health hazard. 'Live' traps are all very well, but you then have to dump the creatures somewhere else. Harden your heart and set lethal spring traps. Also put little containers of poison where rodents can reach but pets and children can't. The best solution? A cat.

42

Rats are real trouble. They can cause material damage and spread really nasty diseases. Act immediately. Put down an effective poison (though see preceding tip). This does work, but if you're squeamish call out the local pest control officer, who'll do it for you. Otherwise, a big farm cat or a good 'ratting' terrier are the best deterrents.

43

Stains from pet urine on the carpet need instant attention. Blot as much as possible with paper towels or (with darker carpets) old newspaper. Tread on top to squeeze out as much as possible. Spray white vinegar sparingly on the area, leave for five minutes and blot again. Repeat the procedure twice more. This should get rid of stain and smell.

44

Even a **microwave oven** can get spattered with food and grease, but **cleaning it could hardly be simpler.** Put in a small bowl or mug of water with a few drops of lemon juice. Shut the door and switch to 'high' for five minutes, so that the steam softens the dirt. Then wipe out the inside with a damp cloth.

45

Vacuum your mattress once a month. This will suck up flakes of dried skin and other detritus which attract and nourish bed bugs and dust mites. Go right into the grooves and bits of piping round the edge. For the same reasons, pull out the bed and vacuum the floor beneath and behind it.

46

Every autumn, check your gutters for debris. Leaves, moss, old nests, mud and grit can block them, causing rainwater to back up and spill over. If you have to use a ladder, lean it against the wall rather than the gutter itself. Hoick out the muck with a trowel, making sure none gets into the downpipe and blocks that instead.

47

If you have airbricks in the external walls, make sure they are clear and clean. Blockages can stop the flow of air under suspended floors, and encourage damp. Tear away weeds and other rubbish, and if necessary clear out the holes in the bricks with a bottle brush or old toothbrush.

48

Your damp course is there for a purpose

– to stop damp rising from the ground into your walls. Soil or other debris piled against the external walls can bridge the damp course, rendering it useless. So check regularly all round the house and remove any build-up.

49

The outside of your house needs cleaning,

just like the inside. Once a year (especially if you live near a busy road) hose down the exterior walls to get rid of mud, dust and exhaust deposits, top to bottom. You may need a pressure hose to reach the very top, but lower the pressure for windows and other delicate parts.

50

Give your outside timber decking a spring clean.

Remove furniture and sweep up leaves and dust. Use an old knife to clear away bits of gunge stuck between the slats. Wash down the wood with diluted oxygen bleach or a similar environmentally-friendly chemical. Finally, wash the whole thing down with a hose.

William Fortt

William Fortt is an environmentalist and as such is an absolute stickler for respecting the things around him, ensuring that they are carefully ordered and well maintained. He has been an author for more than 30 years, with many books to his name, including *The Little Book of Green Tips* (also Absolute Press).

THE LITTLE BOOK OF
BARBECUE
TIPS
ANDREW LANGLEY

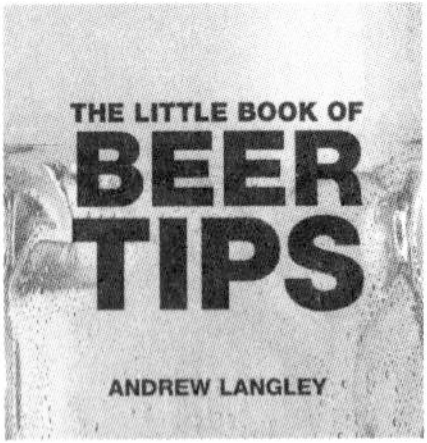
THE LITTLE BOOK OF
BEER
TIPS
ANDREW LANGLEY

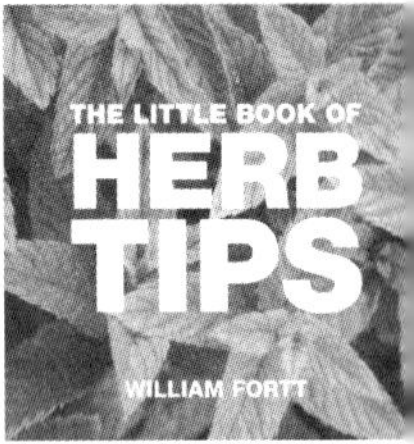
THE LITTLE BOOK OF
HERB
TIPS
WILLIAM FORTT

THE LITTLE BOOK OF
POKER
TIPS

THE LITTLE BOOK OF
GARDENING
TIPS
WILLIAM FORTT

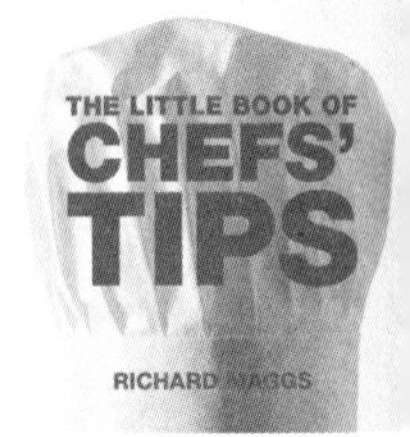
THE LITTLE BOOK OF
CHEFS'
TIPS
RICHARD

THE LITTLE BOOK OF
SPICE
TIPS
ANDREW LANGLEY

THE LITTLE BOOK OF
GOLF
TIPS
PETER FRENCH

THE LITTLE BOOK OF
TIPS
SERIES

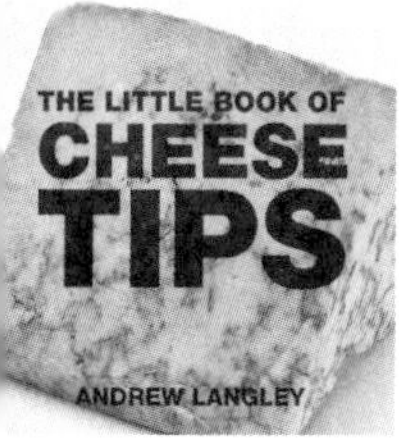
THE LITTLE BOOK OF
CHEESE
TIPS
ANDREW LANGLEY

WINE
TIPS

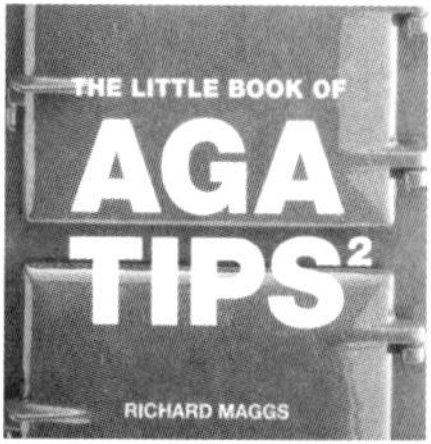
THE LITTLE BOOK OF
AGA
TIPS 2
RICHARD MAGGS

COFFEE
TIPS
ANDREW LANGLEY

THE LITTLE BOOK OF
TEA
TIPS
ANDREW LANGLEY

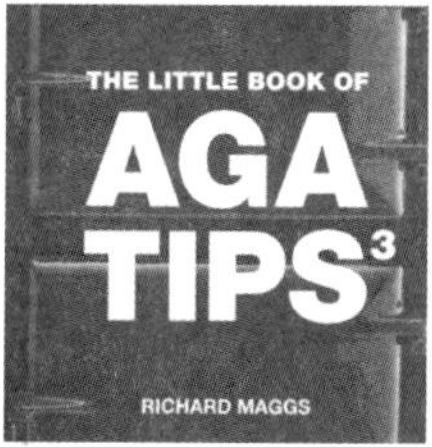
THE LITTLE BOOK OF
AGA
TIPS 3
RICHARD MAGGS

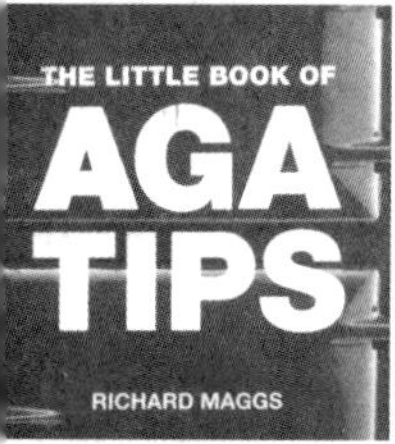
THE LITTLE BOOK OF
AGA
TIPS
RICHARD MAGGS

THE LITTLE BOOK OF
CHRISTMAS
AGA
TIPS
RICHARD MAGGS

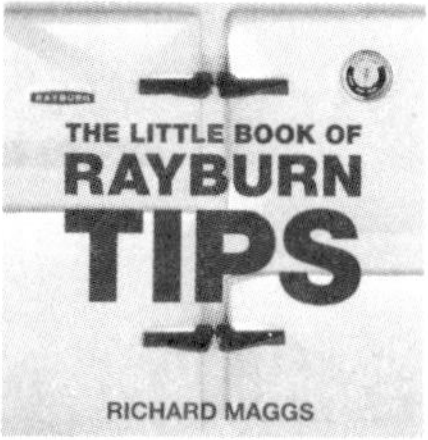
THE LITTLE BOOK OF
RAYBURN
TIPS
RICHARD MAGGS

THE LITTLE BOOK OF
BRIDGE
TIPS
PETER FRENCH

THE LITTLE BOOK OF
CHESS
TIPS
PETER FRENCH

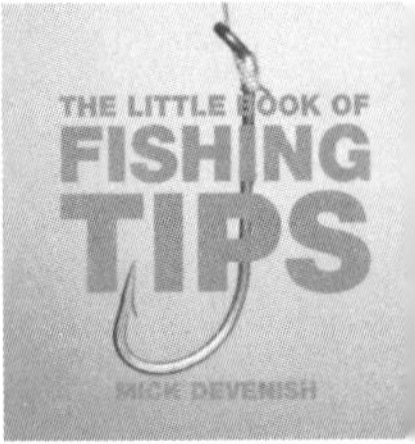
THE LITTLE BOOK OF
FISHING
TIPS
NICK DEVENISH

THE LITTLE BOOK OF
GREEN
TIPS
WILLIAM FORTT

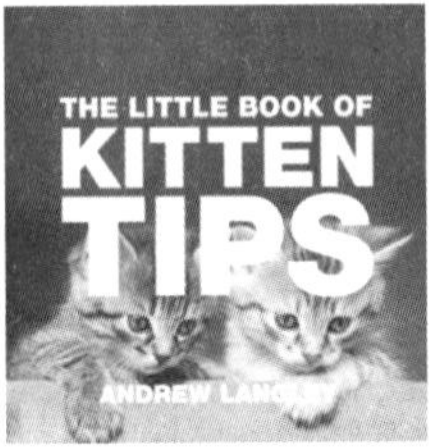
THE LITTLE BOOK OF
KITTEN
TIPS
ANDREW LANG

MARMITE
PAUL HARTLEY
THE LITTLE BOOK OF
MARMITE
TIPS

THE LITTLE BOOK OF
PUPPY
TIPS
ANDREW LANGLEY

THE LITTLE BOOK OF
WHISKY
TIPS
ANDREW LANGLEY

THE LITTLE BOOK OF
TRAVEL
TIPS
MEGAN DEVENISH

Little Books of Tips from Absolute Press

Aga Tips
Aga Tips 2
Aga Tips 3
Allotment Tips
Backgammon Tips
Barbecue Tips
Beer Tips
Biscuit Tips
Bread Tips
Bridge Tips
Cake Baking Tips
Cake Decorating Tips
Cheese Tips
Chefs' Tips
Chess Tips
Chocolate Tips
Christmas Aga Tips
Chutney and Pickle Tips
Cleaning Tips
Cocktail Tips
Coffee Tips
Cupcake Tips
Curry Tips
Fishing Tips
Fly Fishing Tips
Frugal Tips
Gardening Tips
Golf Tips
Green Tips
Grow Your Own Tips
Herb Tips
Houseplant Tips
Ice Cream Tips
Jam Tips
Kitten Tips
Macaroon Tips
Marmite Tips
Olive Oil Tips
Pasta Tips
Poker Tips
Puppy Tips
Rayburn Tips
Seafood Tips
Spice Tips
Tea Tips
Toast Tips
Travel Tips
Whisky Tips
Wine Tips
Vinegar Tips